John— Happy Birthday —
this is to preview a
year's subscription to the
N.Y. The Atlantic Monthly
is frantic over your
lapse. 😊 Love, A

Other **NEW YORKER** *books*

The New Yorker Book of Dog Cartoons (1992)

The Complete Book of Covers from *The New Yorker*,
1925—1989 (1989)

THE
NEW YORKER
BOOK OF CAT CARTOONS

THE NEW YORKER
BOOK OF CAT CARTOONS

ALFRED A. KNOPF ❧ NEW YORK 1995

Library of Congress Cataloging in Publication Data
The New Yorker book of cat cartoons.

p. cm.
ISBN 0-679-74276-X
1. Cats—Caricatures and cartoons. 2. American wit and humor, Pictorial.
3. New Yorker (New York, N.Y.) l. New Yorker (New York, N.Y.)
NC1428.N47 1990
741.5'973—dc20 90-53070
CIP

Manufactured in the United States of America
Published October 25, 1990
First Miniature Paperback Edition Published October 4, 1992
Reprinted Five Times
Seventh Printing, May 1995

THE
NEW YORKER
BOOK OF CAT CARTOONS

"I know a lot of people will say 'Oh, no— not another book about cats.'"

"We had her declawed, but she's still impossible."

"Everyone be home by two o'clock!"

3

NEW, IMPROVED CAT

4

*"But when she got there, the cupboard was bare,
and so the poor dog had none."*

"Guess what we've done. We've just caught a mouse!"

"I've never seen him pause next to anyone longer!"

*"Your wife feels that your cat needs to hear
an authoritative male voice."*

"Am I talking to myself?"

STEINBERG

11

"All right, darling, I promise. No more canned food."

"By the way, I've ordered a cat."

13

"Makes you wonder, doesn't it?"

*"From this day forward, we will do our <u>very</u> <u>best</u> to do unto
Pussy as we would have Pussy do unto us."*

16

O. SOGLOW

"This year I'm just going to give everybody kittens."

MOVIES FOR CATS

20

"One final question: Do you now own or have you ever owned a fur coat?"

ACT   TAC ATC TCA CTA

"It's very simple. If I was a cat, you would love me."

"*Before reading Miss Simpkins' will, may I say that you are a very lucky cat?*"

"*Margo, I think it's time we talked about us.*"

1

2

3

4

*"When she was little, we had a very close relationship,
but now we're just friends."*

"*Around here his word is law.*"

*"One morning they went out for a walk, and
that's the last I ever saw of them."*

31

S.GROSS

32

ST. LOUIS
FAMILY MOVED
LEFT ME BEHIND
BY ACCIDENT

W Miller

"I mean, God, Philip, what if he doesn't really like Tabby Treat but is only eating it so we'll feel less guilty?"

35

"Are you all right?"

*"Of course some cats have eight kittens
but I never have more than six."*

37

"We laugh at the same things."

sempé

"Mrs. Wallace _made_ me take them. She said
they were as much ours as theirs."

"Edgar, please run down to the shopping center right away,
and get some milk and cat food. Don't get canned tuna, or chicken,
or liver, or any of those awful combinations. Shop around
and get a surprise. The pussies like surprises."

41

THE VIGIL

43

Front row: Smarty, Itty Fitty, Daisy, Boo, Mercedes, Foo Foo, Aka.
Second row: Spanky, Charlie, Mouse, Tigger, KiKi, Fluffy, Honey, Jerry.
Third row: Sweetheart, Pumpkin, B.J., Dennis, Emlyn, Pearl, Annie.
Back row: Miss Perringer.

"We're out of the cat food. Permit me to recommend the dog food."

47

"If I take too many naps during the day, I find
it difficult to sleep well at night."

"Well, I hope you're proud of yourself!"

STEINBERG

BUDGIE DEFICIT

53

"*He knows I can't stand it when he doesn't eat.*"

"I've enjoyed our little talk, and now I'll
have myself a nice little nap."

"Like this—see? You've got to get your back into it."

"Is it all right for an expectant mother to catch chipmunks?"

"All right, come out and we'll talk about it."

S.GROSS

61

| TODAY |

Today I got some food in a bowl. It was great! I slept some too.

| TODAY |

Played with yarn. Got some food in a bowl. Had a good nap.

| TODAY |

Slept. food. yarn. Fun!

| TODAY |

I played with a shoelace. Ate. slept. a good day.

| TODAY |

Slept. Ate some food. Yum.

| TODAY |

Food in a bowl. Yarn galore. Dozed for quite a while.

| TODAY |

Had a good nap. Then food in a bowl. Then yarn.

"The fact that you cats were considered sacred in ancient Egypt cuts no ice with me."

"The patient in 12-C needs comforting."

"I distinctly heard a bark."

"*And I can get along without you!*"

"Beg."

"She has her own agenda."

"I tried to make it from the windowsill to the top of the refrigerator. How about you?"

"Well, sir, then I take it you would vote for any cat
in preference to a capable dog."

73

"I believe I've earned the right to your respect."

"Do you think a Siamese cat could tip it over?"

"And whose little mole is this?"

80

Cheney

"What do cats want?"

*"We have fourteen cats, but Kevin thinks
we only have twelve."*

"Don't get cute with me."

Scaredy-Cats

CATS ARE NOT AS INTELLIGENT AS YOU THINK.

"Glendora Hagan got in another load of cats,
Elinor honey. Can you take a couple?"

"Both cats are mad at me."

"Now let's see—there's the Brosnahans, Mrs. Waldo,
Arthur Elder, the man at the A. & P. store. Now I wonder
about Hannah Carpenter."

"Now, don't start complaining till you taste it."

"I said you're in my light."

PUSS IN FACTORY SECONDS

"I'm a Cheshire mouse."

"Muffie's shedding."

"I'm sorry, but I think it's uncatlike."

*"I do apologize, Rinehart. The cat has never
bitten anyone previously."*

"Hey, pal, let's hear 'Doggie in the Window' again, and this time play it like you mean it!"

"Miss Egan, bring me everything we have on cats."

Index of Artists

The text of this book was set in Caslon Old Face No. 2
on a Macintosh IIci. Printed by Halliday Lithographers,
West Hanover, Massachusetts. Bound by Arcata Kingsport, Inc.,
Kingsport, Tennessee.
Designed by Virginia Tan.